What Is It?

by Lada Josefa Kratky

NATIONAL GEOGRAPHIC

School Publishing

Look, Lin. What is it?
It is fog.

You can not see a lot
in the fog.

Look, Lin. Here it is. I can
see it hit. It is not a lot.

Oh no, Lin! Look!
What is this?

What is this? I do not
like it. I can not look.

What is this? I see the
fog go. Can I go?

Go hop on the log, Lin!
I can hop in here. I like it
like this. I like it a lot.